T0196551

Poetry,
MY FIRST LANGUAGE

Poetry,
MY FIRST LANGUAGE

RITA FIDLER DORN

Library of Congress Control Number:		2017901838
ISBN:	Hardcover	978-1-5245-8187-9
	Softcover	978-1-5245-8186-2
	eBook	978-1-5245-8188-6

Print information available on the last page.

Rev. date: 05/01/2018

To order additional copies of this book, contact:
Xlibris
1-888-795-4274
www.Xlibris.com
Orders@Xlibris.com
542811

What Are They Saying About This Book?

"Ricki's poems are warm and personal, sometimes surprisingly revealing. She writes of life and living and memorable moments, of relationships, and the call of Nature. Her poetry often induces me to consider how I feel about similar moments in my own life."

— ***Ron Feldheim***. *Information systems specialist, clinical microbiologist, wordsmith, rational mystic*

"Her poetry has a profound lyrical quality that sings of an understanding of the human spirit and dances on the profundity of experience. In an expression of humor and everyday sentiment, the pages of this book take the reader on a journey of depth and whimsy."

— ***Hannibal Rosa.*** *Composer / musician*

"Once again, as in Strands of Rhyme: Poems from the Real World, Rita Dorn's newest poems pulse with life. Her stanzas are delightful blossoms filled with fragrance. They glow on the page like juicy, blood-red fruit to be knowingly savored. Dorn's powerful writing unfailingly touches the reader: Her words let spirit whisper and love shine like pure gold."

— ***Jo C. Ledakis***. *International conference interpreter, writer, poet, author of Wild Sea-Salt of Life and InNerviews with Soul*

"Rita Fidler Dorn is one of those rare poets who writes not only from the heart but from within the heart. Whether she speaks of remembrances, conflicts, or tattoos, Ricki's poems flow with vitality. They embrace you, knock you for a loop, pick you up and surprise you. Most of all, they infuse you with the joy of life."

— ***Louis K. Lowy***. *Author of these novels: Die Laughing, Pedal, and The Humachine*

These Are Their Words:

"I envy the way Ricki Dorn's poetry connects the words and the dots to evoke the reader's emotions. Ricki's poetic voice touched my heart and soul. She is a passionate poet who has been granted the gift of melding words into poetry."

— **Mort Laitner**. *Attorney, author of* <u>A Hebraic Obsession</u>, <u>The Greatest Gift</u>, *and* <u>The Hanukkah Bunny</u>

"Ricki Dorn's first language is, indeed, poetry. Her work is both down-to-earth and inspirational. Her fresh slant on familiar themes brings insight and wisdom. Plus, she's a joy to read! What more could you ask for? Read her books and experience it all for yourself."

— **Dr. Steve Liebowitz**. *Novelist, poet, life coach*

"Ricki's poems run the gamut from serious to humorous, but there is always a lesson to be gleaned from reading them."

— **Steve Berlin**. *Accountant, reader, traveler, poetry fan*

"Poetry characterized by whimsy infused with passion, surprise, and sentiment is the core of Rita Fidler Dorn's work."

— **Dr. Carol Menthe-Wells**. *International museum exhibiting artist;* and **Dr. Roger Wells**. *Author, inventor*

"Drawing inspiration from family and friends, Ricki Dorn's poems are filled with wit and wisdom. This new book is a celebration of life."

— **Tere Starr**. *Miami Poets Soirée founder, poet*

"Rita's poetry is universally relatable and personally connectable on many levels. Readers will find their own personal interpretations in each ode and that is what she wants. . . for you to make it your own."

— **Eunice Udelf**. *Traveler, teacher, folk dancer, poet, optimist*

TABLE OF CONTENTS

Acknowledgments xiv
Introduction xv
Dedication xvi

POETRY SOUP

Morning Pats My Hand 3
The Time They Inhabit...4
Blueprint 5
Bird Haiku..5
Culture Vulture 6
The Voice of Language...8
Clowns' Fiasco 9
Phone Call From Son 10
The Business of Living 11
Pillow Talk..12

BEAUTY OF THE BEASTS

Amy, the Good Gorilla..17
Bea, the Kissing Gourami 18
Blessing of the Animals 19
Dwight...20
Mariposa 21
Our Canine Family Member..22
Rocking Horse 23
The Turtle..24
Visitor 25

PLACES OF GREAT OR LITTLE NOTE

Chiming for Me 29

South Beach Street Scene 30

January in Miami 31

Key West Duo 32

Lifeblood of America 33

Let the City Inspire You 34

New York Screenshots 36

The Magic of Paris 37

LOVE STORIES

Anniversary Poem 41

She's a Store-Bought Woman 42

Body Parts 43

Be My Sherpa, Too 44

Happy Is 46

When is Love? 47

Jeffrey Peach 48

My Sons 50

My Hero and My Honey 51

The Spark of Love 52

Happy Birthday, America 53

WAR STORIES

Calendar Hill 57

Downtown Double 58

Haiku Hotel: Room 5-7-5 60

It Pains My Soul 61

I Wanted To. 62

Remnants 63

Darkened Soul 64

Ravages of War 66

COLOR YOUR LIFE

American Sentence...71

Worlds of Color...72

Blue & Greens: Blue Funk Mood Music, 3 Greens.........................76

What Do Colors Say?..78

Sky Blue Pink..79

Hours of Yellow...80

NUTRITION? MENU, PLEASE

Ice Cream in the Morning...85

Cookie Crumbs..86

Favorite Food Experiences..87

Ninette..88

Manners Big Boy..89

The Faces of Pizza..90

WEATHER REPORT

Antics of the Wind...95

Hurricane Moves..96

Sitting in the Rain..97

Misty Clouds 98

Rainy Night Reflections..99

The Sea's Agenda..100

Environmental Haiku 101

Wind Traveler..102

Who is the Sun?...103

SOCIAL COMMENTARY

Circle of Influence..107

Street Corner...108

Playground..109

Tattoo Collage 110

Standing on the Fence.. 111

Jewelry Story 112

Trio...113

Thanking + Giving 114

AGE, AGES, & TIME

In My Thoughts.. 119

Summer of My Discontent 120

Wicked Wednesday...122

 Just Tooling Along 123

No, I Won't Go Gently. 124

On Being 70 125

Retire and Wait for Death? 126

Sonnet of Age..127

Remembrance of Things Past 1 and 2 128

The Juggler 130

SELFIES

Don't Break Her Rules 135

I Never Thought That I Was Real..136

Some Days 137

Milestone Birthday...138

Climb into the Bed 139

Roller Coaster 140

ACKNOWLEDGMENTS

I happily acknowledge all of the people who have crossed my path— in friendship, love, and conflict, for they created the fodder for many of these poems. The world at large and my own responses to that world provided the rest. Numerous poems are reflections of my experiences, while some are those of the kind souls who have generously shared their episodes with me. South Florida Writers Association continues to be my staff of literary support and I am grateful for the strength I derive from all of the members, many of whom have become my special, treasured friends.

Specifically, I gratefully acknowledge my editor, Holly Wechsler Schwartztol, Ph.D., for her dedicated efforts with this book. Her critiques and suggestions during the process were helpful and illuminating.

INTRODUCTION

Dear Reader:

I am pleased to share this poetic journey with you. Whether you are new to my poems or are coming back for more, I hope we will have a pleasant writer-reader relationship here. This anthology is both a continuation of and a divergence from my first volume, *Strands of Rhyme: Poems from the Real World*. In contains odes similar to those in *Strands* as well as experimental styles and topics. It is an expansion of my lifelong passion for poetry: writing it, reading it, sharing it, and writing some more. Perhaps this book will motivate the little poet inside of you to write some too. Happy reading!

R.F.D.

DEDICATION

This book is dedicated to my husband, Jeffrey, who tries to stay on the same page with me, often a daunting task. He has been my inspiration, motivation, and appreciation for all I do and all I am.

It is also lovingly dedicated to the memory of my parents, Beatrice and David Fidler, and my brother, Eric Stephan Fidler, all of whom who would have heartily shared my pleasure in the publication of this book.

POETRY SOUP

"Soup is often the starter dish for a meal, and so it will be for this book."

— Rita Fidler Dorn

"To have great poets, there must be great audiences, too."

— Paul Engle (1908-1991)
University of Iowa

"The impulse to enter, with other humans, through language, into the order and disorder of the world, is poetic at its root as surely as it is political at its root. "

— Adrienne Rich,
Academy of American Poets Chancellor
(1999–2001)

MORNING PATS MY HAND

Morning pats my hand softly,
like a kitten reminding its mistress
     of breakfast time.

Morning warms my heart
as quickly as coffee
     filling my big ceramic cup.

It expands;
it is the heat of my rising sun,
     on a sandy beach.

Morning is the diving board of my day,
propelling me toward yet another lap
     of my swim in the pool of life.

THE TIME THEY INHABIT

Some people live in the time they inhabit;
others visit the realm of their past;
those who dare to dwell in the future
are pioneers of progress—
blazing trails,
parting pathways,
inventing, discovering, proposing,
building bridges and
stretching skyways
to everyone's world of tomorrow.

BLUEPRINT

All of us map plans and goals, have hopes and ambitions,
dream dreams and make what we deem are right decisions;
but leave room on your blueprint for some new visions:
adjustments, changes, and radical revisions.

Know that Life doesn't care for your intentions
or what you had planned, as your best inventions;
it puts what It wants into your body and mind,
although you may loathe what you'll find.

You might pound your fist in anger
or or weep tears of piteous sorrow;
but you still must face and cope with
what Life hands you each Tomorrow.

BIRD HAIKU

He   who   closes his

window   will   not   have   a   bird

fly   into   his   house.

CULTURE VULTURE

(spoken word)

culture's not a vulture but reveals the past we've passed.
it's our childhood, family, country, and faith which lasts.
it's our rituals that grow habitual, and all that we profess—
human and unique, who we are: no more, no less.

culture could be a high-falluting fling;
it's an everyone-does-it-differently thing.
like attending the opera, in a fancy hall on the hill
or having a nanny, if you live in brazil.

it's going fishing if your home's near a lake,
and duck-watching to catch sight of a drake.
it's taking the bus if you live in inner city
and private jokes only your crowd finds witty.

it's a fire of belief, with no desire for relief;
it's treasure and pleasure—like standing still on a reef.
culture tells how we were raised
and with what games we were hazed.

it's what parents told us to do and what we couldn't.
it's what we dared to, especially if warned we shouldn't.
it's who you are when you are part of a group,
and the selfie you show, when home alone, eating soup.

it's your inner and your outer, your smiler and your pouter,
your accepter and your doubter.
inspired or acquired, when your lining's wired;
your vitality— not yet expired.

culture is our mind and brain, with contentment and disdain;
it's the skin we're in, when we lose or win—it's a loud refrain.
it's the face we show the world, when calm or in turmoil.
culture's not a vulture. no,   not   at   all.

THE VOICE OF LANGUAGE

Language is the expression of your innermost thoughts,
traveling directly from your soul.
It's like a baby emerging from the womb,
to make its way in the world.

Language connects you to the minds and hearts
of your fellow living creatures.
Words are tentacles which
validate themselves, by reaching out.

Verbally, the sounds and syllables
are instant gratification for you.
But, no sooner spoken, they evaporate. . .
leaving only their messages behind.

In print, words achieve some immortality
which can be revisited, pondered, and shared.

Language speaks in many tongues:
dance, music, art—accessible to all ethnicities.
Gardening, architecture, athletics, as well,
contribute to the global conversation.

With the glorious gift of language,
we can pull strings from our own minds,
and tie them to the existence of others,
anywhere in the universe.

CLOWNS' FIASCO

A wintertime heist
in a jewelry store;
clerks were all worried
that they'd be beaten and sore.

The temperature rose
and heartbeats quickened.
The criminals were clowns.
The plot thickened.

They dealt bills like cards to one another
and juggled shiny coins of gold.
Pretty soon everyone's
anxiety grew a little bit cold.

The police arrived but
alas, all too late;
the clowns had departed
—they could not wait.

They took a few rings
as their mementos,
eating lunch on the run—
green olive sandwiches with pimentos.

This happened in a chilly December,
truly a fiasco to remember.

PHONE CALL FROM SON

Son called his mom:
"Just wanted to say
have a beautiful day;
in the car now, on my way
  to the place where I work
  at my job as a law clerk,
  and my boss, a cool Turk.
I recall you cooked many a pot
of veggie soups, tasty and hot,
which we all loved and ate a lot.
  So be careful and keep feeling well--
  don't want news that you fell.
  I love you, Mom, and think you're swell."

THE BUSINESS OF LIVING

The business of living means
dealing with ghosts from the past,
preparing for the future,
and negotiating the complex super highways
of the present.

Seeking an even keel
between depression and euphoria.
Money: earn some, save some, spend some joyfully.
Pay the bills, but buy a few thrills.

Attempting to harmonize relationships?
Participate, support, enjoy. . . . but become not their slaves.
Cherish the healthy days and address those that aren't, as best you can.
Don't obsess or make body maintenance a full time occupation.

Just live. Seek satisfaction. Pay your dues.
Hard to find that middle road and balance on it squarely.
But, try. That is the business of living.

PILLOW TALK

AT THE CRIB
      small sounds of love,
      verbalized visions of the future
      words to the infant, years before it can understand; baby coos.
      syllables of joy, fear, awe, hope, plus tiny kisses.

SIBLINGS' CHILDHOOD WHISPERS
      from bed to bed or room to room, late at night
      above downstairs living room sounds of adults
      or in the sleepy morning, before anyone else has awakened,
      as warm fingers of sunshine seep in through the window.

SUMMER CAMP NOCTURNES
      in tent or cabin, on bunks or cots,
      hear secrets brought from distant cities;
      gossip, sexy tidbits, ghost stories.
      country breezes cool the words.

SLEEPOVERS WITH BEST FRIENDS
      revealing treasured pearls of information
      from the sea-depths of teenage hearts
      to the only qualified recipients—
      8th grade soul-mates, now BFFs

DORM ROOMIES
      intense, focused, urgent, clever, hilarious.
      the oatmeal topics of college conversations:
      grades, heart throbs, money, life, family;
      politics, the world, the future; fears, tears, anticipation.

WITH LOVERS

    before or after sex, soft, slow, relaxed.

    emotions, observations. easy, random, ambling.

    a little bit of touching— preamble or leftovers.

    savoring the silver intimacy of those moments.

HOSPITAL ROOM

    weak whispered words, raspy efforts, both wanting to say more.

    "I love you" is in there someplace.

    small sentences; pats on the head and hands.

    lies, truths, regrets, promises, goodbyes.

BEAUTY OF THE BEASTS

"The greatness of a nation and its moral progress can be judged by the way its animals are treated."

— Mahatma Gandhi

"Until one has loved an animal, a part of one's soul remains unawakened."

— Anatole France

"Such short little lives our pets have to spend with us, and they spend most of it waiting for us to come home each day."

— John Grogan

Amy, the Good Gorilla

written about the main character in Michael Crichton's novel, Congo

Hi, I'm Amy, and I'm a good gorilla.
You have made your language mine,
so now we can communicate—
you speak to me and, in response, I sign.

Sign language is the bond we share;
I wear my knowledge like a royal cape.
We conversationally romp on the island
that bridges the seas of man and ape.

When I want some love or attention, I sign,
"I'm Amy, good gorilla.
Let's take a walk; give me hug;
ice cream please? I like vanilla."

Together we trekked in the heat of the Congo,
with research our common goal;
you are my teacher, my mentor, my friend,
and I play the good student's role.

I'm Amy, and I'm a smart gorilla—
I know someday we'll have to part.
You'll return to your country without me,
and I'll sign to my babies the love in my heart.

I'm Amy and I'm a good gorilla.

BEA, THE KISSING GOURAMI

A kissing gourami whose name was Bea

kissed every fish that she could see.

She kissed the plants and she kissed the tank;

she kissed what floated and what sank.

She kissed the rock, that was painted blue.

She kissed the big plecostomus too.

Bea was the queen of the tropical fish;

Bea was a sweetie, a come-true wish.

With her pink, round belly

and her silvery fins,

the Miss Friendly Fish Contest

she always wins.

She kissed the thermometer

and the fishlets so wee;

when I dropped in some food,

she even kissed me!

BLESSING OF THE ANIMALS

Dear God,

We ask Your merciful blessing for our devoted pets,
for us as their care-takers, and, of course, for the vets.

    The fine, friendly horses, for their devotion,
    for their shiny coats, and speedy locomotion.

For cats and for dogs, for kittens and puppies,
for those who are water-bound, like goldfish and guppies.

    For turtles and hamsters and each furry bunny…
    we give thanks for their loyalty and antics so funny.

For the birds fully feathered, with their gossipy chatter,
and their beautiful colors, whose shades surely flatter.

    For the serpent family, those long, flexible snakes,
    who have such a bad rap—let's give them a break.

For bugs like the ants who crash our picnics with glee,
the spiders who weave, and the sociable bee.

    For the pets in our homes and the beasts in the wild—
    protect them, provide food, let them prosper and smile.

For all of Your critters, the large and the small,
we ask Your Loving Kindness; bless them one and all.

DWIGHT

a condolence note

So sad for the demise of your pet snake,

whom you named Edna but turned out to be Dwight;

hard for both of you that he got sick,

week in and week out, by day and by night.

You were close friends

for 20 sweet years;

hope that only good memories

will shine through your tears.

MARIPOSA

Mariposa spreads her wings of generosity, hospitality, and grace, delightedly displaying their evening gown colors; she is ready for a cotillion and all the guests who have come to pay tribute to her royal highness, as she holds court in the most lush garden of the mansion-owner's property. He appreciates her visits and never fails to praise her vivid attributes to visiting dignitaries who appreciate horticultural excellence. Often they have traveled from distant points to murmur compliments about her rainbow spectrum, glistening steadily in the mist of the afternoon's solar gold. *Mariposa* never fails to thrill on these social occasions. The mansion-owner derives vicarious credit for the beauty of this spec- tacu- lar crea- ture.

Our Canine Family Member

This precious relationship
lasted for many long years;
we'll recall you, dear doggie,
with our smiles and our tears.

Your friendship and loyalty
were devoted and true.
Mornings and evenings,
we still think of you:

Those backyard frolics
and brisk walks in the park,
play wrestling at home;
snacks, biscuits, dinner at dark.

Our four-legged tail-wagger
you were a dear family member,
one whom, with love in our hearts,
we shall always remember.

ROCKING HORSE

The rocking horse I ride every day
takes me to places far away:
lands I've heard about in bedtime tales
or saw in my dreams of India, China, and Wales.

To a big, sandy beach with my pail, shovel, and hoop,
to a forest with creatures who twitter and whoop,
a rough riding sailboat whose canvas is puffy,
choo-chooing trains, their smoke dark and fluffy.

I hop on with excitement as I mount,
off to more magic spots than I can count;
toward castles and dragons and kings and queens,
the good and the evil, and all in between.

Adventures I'll remember all of my life,
even when I grow up and have kids and a wife.
My rocking horse is my very best friend;
he's the buddy on whom I can depend.

THE TURTLE

I am like a turtle;
I keep a hard facade on the outside
to protect my body and my feelings,
but on the inside I am soft.

Sometimes I am overwhelmed by
bigger, bolder, louder residents
who share my environment.

When I am frightened or worried,
I pull myself inside my shell and stay alone,
content with my own good company.

When I am happy and feel brave,
I stick my head out, look around, and
smile at the world.

I like making friends with others of my ilk—
my size, temperament, and similar political views;
with them, I feel safe and accepted, loved and respected.

I don't move very fast, but I keep plugging along.
Remembering Aesop, who said,
"Slow and steady wins the race."

I am in no hurry to finish.
The journey is what it is all about, anyhow,
not the destination.

VISITOR

One sunny morning,

we looked out of our sliding glass living room window

to see a visitor—

a tall, white, heron standing in our backyard pond.

Perfectly still, majestic, calm.

We admired his beauty and grace, his plump midsection,

and slender stick-thin legs.

He glanced at us and retreated out of sight.

Still smiling at his loveliness, we then noticed

the untypical stillness of the pond water,

all of the goldfish missing.

PLACES OF GREAT OR LITTLE NOTE

"What strange phenomena we find in a great city; all we need do is stroll about with our eyes open. Life swarms with innocent monsters."

— *Charles Baudelaire*

"Cities were always like people, showing their varying personalities to the traveler....Only through travel can we know where we belong or not, where we are loved, and where we are rejected."

— *Roman Payne,*
Cities & Countries

"What is the city but the people?"

— *William Shakespeare*, **Coriolanus**

CHIMING FOR ME

Big Ben is chiming only for me;
he knew I would get here eventually.
He has been waiting for me ever since
I wrote my first research paper in 10th grade
on this British icon.

I introduce myself, wanting so much to be friends.
The Westminster Chimes ring loud and true,
resounding clearly.
His voice is deeper than I thought it would be
and his hands pointier.
I marvel at his body, the elegant
Gothic building that supports him.
I view him from two sides on the street and
that night, in awe, from across the Thames River.

Visible from distant miles, regal and historical,
he benevolently surveys his city.
I try to take it all in and keep it
so I will remember everything about him
when I get home.

SOUTH BEACH STREET SCENE

Elderly people sit in shabby, white-webbed lawn chairs
on the sidewalk in front of
their tiny South Beach apartments,
drinking brown iced tea,
counting visits of the green rescue trucks,
heralded by screaming sirens.

"That's the fourth one today," an old woman says.
"Yeah, and they took Bertie, yesterday,"
chimes in a short, wrinkled man.
"Edith's not coming back, you know."
"We know."

They squint in the sunshine,
wiping sweat off creased brows,
all of them wondering
when it will come for them,
in one neighborhood,
on South Beach.

January in Miami

January in Miami is when we remember
snow storms up north in chilly November.
Tropical weather here couldn't be better;
we might need a jacket or maybe a sweater.

Wearing big boots is but a memory fond,
as we gaze, barefoot, across a plant-edged pond.
Inside gloves were once chilly fingers—
now a warm outlook that spreads and lingers.

Not skidding on roads covered with ice;
mere medians with palm trees— sunny and nice.
Nor icicles on house window panes,
no drifts turned to slush whenever it rains.

In January, we smile to recall
a December holiday with no snow at all.
This first month brings a healthier fate:
January's winter sees arthritis abate.

So Miami in January is the place to reside
for swimming, sun tans, and South Florida pride!

KEY WEST DUO

1.   Pebbles in my shoes
    sand between my toes
    drinks at Mallory Square
    as down the sunset goes.

    In Key West— relax, refresh
    a getaway for two
    so glad the other person
    here with me is you.

2.   Duval Street is jumping like Mexican beans,
    sounds and smells both assaulting and stimulating tourists
    in Key West for a respite from their own drama.
       Boutiques with high priced goods sit beside shops
       which display tacky T-shirts and souvenirs of every variety.

    Myriads of restaurants post their menus as far forward
    as the street to entice visitors who are hungry, thirsty, tired,
    lonely, or bored. Music calls out. Even at night humidity persists;
       air conditioned guest house or motel too many blocks away.
       Everybody's sweat walks with the crowd.

    New tattoo? Body pierce? Beer?
    Taxi? Motor scooter? Pedi-cab?
    Girls? Guys? A show?
       A dozen ways to leave your money in old Key West
       as your footprint in the sand.

LIFEBLOOD OF AMERICA

The lifeblood of America is composed of
the songs, the sweat, the sacrifices of the workers.
> It envelopes their values, traditions, and rituals,
> their hopes and goals, persistence and endurance.

The lifeblood of America stands on the foundation of
the cultures, languages, and religions of the workers.
> It flows through their bodies, minds, and souls,
> and navigates their pinnacles and plummets.

Keep the lifeblood flowing through America's veins,
through her banks and libraries, her farms and factories,
schools and museums, hospitals and stores.
> Let it flow through her streets and rivers,
> offices and theaters, airports and bus stations,
> football fields and coffee shops, rose gardens and parking lots.

The workers are the lifeblood of America.
> All that they wish for,
> all that they are, America is.
> They are America.

LET THE CITY INSPIRE YOU

Look at the office buildings, sleek and tall, and wonder about the
    myriad of lives and tasks they contain—
    efforts, frustration, successes within their confines;
    sound of elevators, computer clicks, fax machines.

Stare at each walker pacing the sidewalks in sandals, sneakers, loafers,
    oxfords, pumps, flats, and boots, covering urban miles;
    ponder their destinations.

Meet eyes with diners inside a restaurant, having scored window seats
    and relishing their meals, but glancing outside to the street,
    mid-course. For a millisecond, you are intimates; conjure up
    appropriate culinary aromas.

See shoppers emerge from the stores, laden with colored bags bannered
    with logo and company name. What acquisitions will be added to
    closet, kitchen, family room, bedroom? How will each newcomer
    adapt to its new home?

Spot each passing car, bus, taxi, bike, entering your view but escaping
    right away, bent on arriving. . . .someplace, each with its
    time-conscious human cargo. Speculate.

Greet the street cleaners, beggars, loiterers, bag-people, pushcart vendors—
another segment of the *dramatis personae* of the city; they too
have their magic, their network.

Smile at the doves searching for a few crumbs of bread, at the tree branches
waving, at the benevolent feel of wind and sunshine.

The city and its inhabitants move, seemingly at will, but are actually
fenced within. What heartbeats and aspirations accompany each
player in the theatre of the city? What personal music does
each one hear? Hear it too.

NEW YORK SCREENSHOTS

New York is "the city that never sleeps,"
but it mourns and weeps;
it sings, sways, and dances;
it gambles and takes crazy chances.

A place to be discovered,
lose your identity or have it recovered.
Seek your fortune in this town—
the stocks go up; the stocks go down.

Museums, restaurants, and shops galore.
You'll see it all: the ravenously rich and abject poor.
"Give my regards to Broadway,"
an evening show or a matinee!

The music of New York City
shows the power of vast ethnicity.
A downtown to visit, a place to reside,
a culture with which one may abide.

Have an affair with this historic town.
Fall in love with life here; it won't let you down!

THE MAGIC OF PARIS

The magic of the city, the sparkle of the wine, walking the Champs Elysees, stopping for *sorbet avec Grand Marnier* half way; we peep into store windows, pristine and ocean clear.

History of long ago centuries hails us with *"Bienvenue à Paris!"* We reply *"Merci,"* unearthing high school French, with a few updates from the phrase book purchased at the airport.

We peer up at the sky through the millions of struts
of the Eiffel Tower, dutifully awed by its size and history.

Electronic device charging stations at the airport reinforce on-time arrival of the age of technology, at Gate 4. We are greeted by an automated passport scanning machine!

What a difference from the gruff customs officers on whom we could practice our rusty, limited *français,* hoping not to be singled out for a crisp "Unlock your suitcase, please."

The Louvre's enormous lobby opens its arms to the tourists we are that day. Mona Lisa and Venus de Milo welcome us to their home; the works of Raphael, Rubens, Michelangelo, Caravaggio, and Bosch surpass their reputations.

Pedalers on bicycles nod to us cheerily. Ranks of marching school children shyly acknowledge our smiles. Sunny day.

The vivid oil paintings on the walls of our flat in the artsy *Marais* district welcome us back, each evening, on our weary and happy return to our temporary digs.

Love Stories

"Friends show their love in times of trouble, not of happiness."

— *Euripides*

"Spread love everywhere you go. Let no one ever come to you without leaving happier."

— *Mother Teresa*

"Love is when the other person's happiness is more important than your own."

— *H. Jackson Brown, Jr.*

"What's the stuff of which love is made? Ingredients, durability, guarantee, magic? Pretty elusive. It's all around town, but hard to pin down."

— *R.F. Dorn*

ANNIVERSARY POEM

On the day we said "I do,"
I gave my earnest vow to you

that we'd stand close in sickness and health
as well as poverty and wealth,
and on the days that we would laugh
plus those that broke our hearts in half;
with successes that we won
and losses that weren't any fun.

I said it then; I mean it still.
I love you with all my heart;
and I always will.

SHE'S A STORE-BOUGHT WOMAN

"I'm a store bought woman, but not the kind you think.
Not given to Cracklin' Rose or any spirit-filled drink.
I'm a store bought woman but not one of ill repute;
love to hear praise and that my honey thinks I'm cute.

I look at girls in lindsey-woolsey or simple calico frocks,
Mary Janes on their feet to dance in, 'til the church floor rocks.
But that's not me; I like it fancy, not plain,
and anything other, I view with distain.

I want silk and satin and diamonds and pearls.
I love my stylist to put my hair up in curls;
yearn to be taken to the best spots in town,
my body wrapped up in a custom made gown.

I'm a store bought woman, no taste for made at home;
desire goods from big city stores: golden hairbrush, silver comb.
I deliver what I promise — I'm not a tease;
you can count on it, sweetie; I know how to please."

BODY PARTS

Your locks are straight,
your eyes are forgiving,
your smile is soft.

      Your shoulders are broad,
      your back is smooth,
      your chest is hairy.

Your thighs are solid,
your calves are sculpted,
your ankles are trim.

      Your arms are enveloping,
      your soul is sweet,
      your heart is mine.

BE MY SHERPA, TOO

(with appreciation to Andrew Varnon)

Be my sherpa,
be my first ray of sunshine in the morning
be my breakfast in bed.

Be the birds singing outside our window
be the smell of fresh gardenias in an English garden
be the taste of Earl Grey tea
be my rainbow.

Be my holding hands
be the little voice inside of me,
be my second set of eyes
be the word on the tip of my tongue,
be my push to go the extra mile.

Be my "let's kick it up a notch"
be my "hills are alive with the sound of music"
be my "shelter from the storm"
be my "sound of silence"
be my "more than the greatest love the world has known."

Be the book we both loved reading
be the same page we both are on
be my punch line.

Be my "grow old along with me"
be my "autumn leaves" in fall
be the "raindrops" that "keep falling on my shoulder"
be my "Johnny Angel"
be my "76 trombones"
be my parade that nobody can rain on.

44

Be my "we're going to get through this, honey"
be my "maybe there's another way to look at it"
be your arm around my shoulder when I say, "Make it not hurt so much."

Be my fireplace in winter, be the twinkle in my eye
be my good deed, be my touch of class,
be the levels I thought I could never reach.

You already are, and it has made all the difference.

HAPPY IS . . . .

Happy is an ice cream cone on an oven-hot day
or steaming vegetable soup on a snowy night

going to see a football game
or seeing your team win

not needing an operation
or surviving an operation

waking up and not having the flu
or just waking up.

Happy is sleeping late, not having to go to work
or getting up early, grateful to have a job

finding out you are not pregnant
or finding out you are

sharing a joke
or exchanging a glance

falling in love with life, with a passion, with your own confidence
or finding your soul mate, who was looking for you.

Happy are hours spent with a cherished grandparent,
enjoying time with your adult children,
playing with a precious grandchild.

Being loved by many
being loved by those who count.

WHEN IS LOVE?

Love is when you share a deep glance,
a dreamy dance,
a rakish romance.

It's when you laugh and cry
under sun or a rainy sky
but won't say goodbye.

It's when it feels good inside,
you swallow your pride,
refuse to hide.

It's when your heart is aglow
and you don't say no,
—just "Let's go."

It's when you know it's right,
every day and night,
in sound and sight.

It's when it's worth it
to birth it,
determinedly unearth it.

It's when you
have the last clue
that it's true for you.

JEFFREY PEACH

Jeffrey Peach,
you are the beach:
     the sun, the surf, the tide;
you are poetry and wine,
a moment stopped in time,
     the crazy top-of-the-ferris-wheel ride!

You love portraits done in antique oil,
bronze statues dug from ancient soil,
     candles flamed in historical yellow.
You tend your garden of herbs and spices,
carefully worship the sun, at a price.
     Man, art, and nature blend to a state of mellow.

Jeffrey Peach,
you are the beach:
     the sun, the surf, the sand;
irresistible,
undismissable,
     Peter Pan in Neverland.

You are joy and chance,
passion and romance,
     my rainbow in every sky;
brightly glittering,
alert and flickering,
     you're an endless, timeless high.

Jeffrey Peach,
you are the beach:
　　　　the sun, the surf, the tide;
unexplainable,
unrestrainable,
　　　　my precious top-of-the-ferris-wheel ride!

MY SONS

So alike but so different;
both are tall and slim;
one is blonde with friendly, green eyes;
one has brown hair and steady eyes as brown as mine.

Both are creative:
one is an artist; he draws shoes.
the other designs computer stuff
and always laughs, except when he's hurting.

One explodes with anger, passion, and purpose,
justifying himself to the world;
one keeps his feelings very deep inside,
and rarely drops the mask.

One became a black belt to stay fit and to protect himself.
the other one pursues extreme sports to
connect with the earth.

Verbal and articulate, both of them write well,
—their legacies from me.
Each sees the world from his unique perspective.

They are like me and so much like each other,
but each is distinctive.
No longer my little boys—now they are men.

MY HERO AND MY HONEY

You find my phone and my keys for me;
I remember the names of all the people at the party.

You do the research for a new vehicle;
I negotiate at the dealership.

You clean up the kitchen sometimes;
I organize your sweater drawer.

You put gas in my car and remind me to take my vitamins;
I urge you to become a vegetarian, too.

You play classical music and read rare books;
I watch Judge Judy.

You tell me to get the extravagant piece of jewelry;
I parallel park, cajoling the car into a tight spot.

You balance the checkbook and answer hard Jeopardy questions;
I write you a poem.

You say, "I love you."
I say, "I love you back."

We are a great team;
you are my hero and my honey.

THE SPARK OF LOVE

Of what is love made?
What ignites that spark?
A look, a touch, a thought,
one together moment,
the perfect word, or a concurred opinion.
A deep embrace, a soft caress,
a kiss, brief or lingering.

A piece of music shared and savored.
A re-opened topic of discussion.
A solution to a challenge.
A golden triumph.
One smile and a responding one.
An aroma, fresh or treasured.

What kindles the spark,
keeps it glowing,
or puts it at risk to go dark?
Nobody knows.
Hard to define,
but bask in the sparkle of it anyhow,
as long as it brightens your life.

HAPPY BIRTHDAY, AMERICA

Happy birthday, America, the home of the red, white, and blue.

On this 4th day of July, solemnly, we salute you!

We remember the battlefields where the red of blood was shed,

signaling the injured's pain and commemorating the dead.

White flowers symbolize perfection. Ivory tulips on each grave

remind us to respect the lives those men and women gave.

They wore well-pressed uniforms, some in snappy navy blue;

the azure of the ocean gleams, where they sailed on vessels true.

Our flag bears stripes of crimson and white and stars on a field of blue;

so on this Independence Day, we say to America, "Happy Birthday to you!"

WAR STORIES

"I am at peace with God. My conflict is with Man."
— *Charlie Chaplin*

"Whenever you're in conflict with someone, there is one factor that can make the difference between damaging your relationship and deepening it. That factor is attitude."
— *William James*

"The hottest place in Hell is reserved for those who remain neutral in times of great moral conflict."
— *Martin Luther King, Jr.*

"You can out-distance that which is running after you, but not what is running inside you."
— *Rwandan Proverb*

"War takes place on many battlefields, not only those in distant lands. Other scenes of fighting, tears, disappointment, and conflict are home, office, school, family, heart, and behind closed doors."
— *Rita Fidler Dorn*

CALENDAR HILL

the weekends trudge down calendar hill
without a visit; without a call.
ending of summer, beginning of fall.
closing of autumn, start of the cold;
this separation is getting old.

being punished for something they did?
or something they said?
just like with no supper putting
naughty kids to bed.
have no idea why.
they just cry and cry.

sometimes they're angry, other times sad.
who is the one who is really "bad"?
who's in charge? what's going on here?
they're not at fault. hell, let's have a beer.

then why are they taking this shabby abuse?
there is no possible excuse.
they should walk out and close the door
and hope it hurts him, right to the core.

the weekends keep trudging down calendar hill
days and weeks are using up their fill—
soon there will be no more left.
just them, all alone, feeling bereft.

attitudes sour and moods now miffed
at a person who's deeply missed,
but he is not the same guy any more.
they need to leave and slam that door!

DOWNTOWN DOUBLE

You're a downtown double,
can't you stay out of trouble
for a couple of days, at least
'till your baby comes home from the hospital?
a good prognosis,
but it was a tricky diagnosis.

now, behave yourself and be the guy
who fell in love with the i—
the girl who used to be me.

i know we've both changed
but don't be estranged;
we're grown-ups now,
and should have learned how
to put some order to our lives.

it doesn't much hurt
not to gamble and lose your shirt
and follow the rules, just a little bit.
so put down that 10th beer
and get your act in gear;
come back to me soon
so we both can sleep better at night.

you're a downtown double—
can't you stay out of trouble?

lay off the chicks
and their porno flicks
and all the stuff you sniff and smoke
and blowing your paycheck,
saying "what the heck!—
i'll do as i please or i'll choke."

you were my man
i know you still can
be part of the family
we once planned.

so, come back to me
and reconnect to the family tree
in the garden of our life.
we have one more chance to do this right;
let's fix it now, while we still can.

HAIKU HOTEL: ROOM 5-7-5

realizing for the

first time, that we are not on

the same page, at all.

missing a phone call

I waited for, but then not

wanting to call back.

feeling sweet, then feel-

ing sour, then not wanting

to feel anymore.

It Pains My Soul

When I have an issue that pains my soul,
like a sword stabbing its victim,
I tend to wallow in the misery
like a little pig in a muddy puddle on the farm.

I sit there, inching the cocoon of entitlement around me,
posting my sign, SUFFERER,
not so much for others to see
but for me to feel.

In my head, I replay the details,
the conversations that hurt,
the malicious intent of the ones who hold me captive
by neglect, indifference, or conflict.

I know this is not healthy.
There are only two correct ways to respond:
fix it or forget it!
Tried the first; failed.

Can't execute the second.
Can't or won't? Not sure which.
Am a little piggy wallowing in the mud, but with
an electric wire attached to me, giving me shocks of agony.

"I won't let this tenant rent space in my life,"
are the words I need to say.

I Wanted To. . . .

I wanted to share my day but you were busy

I wanted to share my pain but you weren't home

I wanted to share the fun I had but you were in a meeting

I wanted to hear your voice but you didn't pick up your phone

I wanted to be closer to you but you kept the space between us

I wanted to get a phone call from you but I didn't

I wanted you to care for me, care about me,

     worry for me, cry with me, rejoice with me, laugh with me

Now I don't try anymore and you don't notice

Now I don't care anymore, but it still hurts.

REMNANTS

your restlessness i ache to soothe, but know i can't. . .

i see your hurts and open wounds that you staunchly,

      sometimes by silence, pretend you've learned to live with

wondering if we are any more than a mirage in the desert

how gently you treat other people's feelings,

      each application a work of art

verbal fencing; nicks but no bloodshed

misunderstanding, but understanding all too well

love means your soul has found its home

you could be the leaves on my emotional tree

which lonely brick are you in the pyramid of my existence?

DARKENED SOUL

"Hello," you say.
"Hello," I answer.
"How are you?" you ask.
"Fine," I lie.
"Looking good," you say.
"Thanks," I smile.
But I'm not fine. Not feeling fine behind my smile,
not looking good under the clothes and the moisturizer
and the makeup and the hairspray.

My body is fighting with my mind.
Mind trying to organize it.
Body trying to survive in the world: doctor visits, aches and pains
but not too many, just enough for them to let me know they are there,
permanent residents. Tests, scans, prescriptions, results of tests,
new meds. Carefully worded diagnoses.
They think I don't get it. How dare they?

Mind tried to remember stuff; give up and write it down,
and then can't find the piece of paper. Sometimes I make same list
several times. Then I feel harassed by all the lists, so I condense them
and get confused. Crumple them up and throw them away.
Start again. Clean paper. Neat handwriting at first, but getting messy.
Starting over, this time calling forth obedient letters on the computer.
Looks better. Easy to prioritize.

Mornings are fairly energetic once I pull myself out of bed,
Theodore Roethke style, "and take my waking slow," as in his poem,
"*The Waking.*" Attack the day before it attacks me.
My list, my stuff, my meds, some makeup, some clothes. All OK.
OK stays for awhile and then takes off, leaving me with darkened soul,
ignoring my blessings, of which people keep reminding me.

"Some people have it worse," they say.
"Sure they do," I answer, "but their having it worse
doesn't help me."

Yes, the blessings are there and I acknowledge them justly,
but they don't neutralize the curses, the deficits, the mistakes,
the bad luck, the offenses, the insults, the neglects, the hurts,
the wrongs, the inequalities, and all the stuff I did not deserve.

The missing pieces leave their irregular shapes, empty, naked,
unfilled, in the jigsaw puzzle of my life.

RAVAGES OF WAR

Military war protects the country, but endangers the soldiers;
it preserves boundaries, but severs families;
it strengthens the economy, but injures bodies.
War's benefits can't be acquired without very expensive cost.
Victory is powerful, but defeat is devastating.

They leave their innocence and idealism abroad,
bringing home souvenirs of artificial limbs and PTSD.
How can we support our nation without losing our
healthy, young men and women to war's ravenous jaws?

For the ones who gave the ultimate,
we will remember them with love.

Those who made profound personal sacrifice
deserve deep respect and gratitude for keeping America
"the land of the free and the home of the brave."

Welcome them back with more than parades and flowers;
offer patience, understanding, and opportunity to rebuild their
fractured and often fragmented lives.
That is our way to be patriotic.

COLOR YOUR LIFE

"I look to a day when people will not be judged by the color of their skin, but by the content of their character."
— *Martin Luther King, Jr.*

"Your attitude is like a box of crayons that color your world. Constantly color your picture gray, and your picture will always be bleak. Try adding some bright colors to the picture by including humor, and your picture begins to lighten up."
— *Allen Klein*

"Sunset is still my favorite color, and rainbow is second."
— *Mattie Stepanek*

"The soul becomes dyed with the color of its thoughts."
— *Marcus Aurelius*

"Color is the keyboard, the eyes are the harmonies, the soul is the piano with many strings. The artist is the hand that plays, touching one key or another, to cause vibrations in the soul."
— *Wassily Kandinsky*

"The information encoded in your DNA determines your unique biological characteristics, such as sex, eye color, age, and Social Security number."
— *Dave Barry*

AMERICAN SENTENCE

Concept was the 17-syllable brainchild of Alan Ginsburg,
but these couplets are mine, created from his principle.

Pink of a sunset, of fragrant roses;
sunburned cheeks; runny noses.

Greige blends grass and farm wheat;
it's the skin of a drum, pulsed out to a beat.

Midnight water delivers
silver slivers to countryside rivers.

WORLDS OF COLOR

the WHITE of bed sheets
crisp and sweet,
the ivory of piano keys'
melodic beat.

WHITE is a wedding gown
in radiance aglow,
or pale, ashen agony,
when a dear one falls low.

YELLOW is laughter
of eyes and of heart—
the feeling of triumph
or of a new start.

YELLOW is a baby's smile
and the toot of a little horn;
tea roses, sunbeams,
calico cloth well-worn.

ORANGE is sunset,
adrift in the sky;
cantaloupe, apricots,
pumpkins not in a pie.

thanksgiving is ORANGE,
and a mood very bright—
blazes and mazes and
up reading all night.

ORANGE is the energy
of fighting a duel,
reflecting, deflecting,
resisting what's cruel.

RED is vibrant and violent,
blood and death;
or the strength of emotion
beneath passionate breath.

fierce flames, energy,
the rebel's fight.
RED is forever, adventure,
and knowing you're right.

GREEN is the grass,
soft under bare feet;
GREEN is jealousy's
relentless heat.

envy, repulsion,
mold and decay…
but GREEN are flower stems
each summer day.

BLUE are the heavens
amassed up above,
or the depression of
unhappy love.

BLUE is the twinkle
of a fine diamond stone;
yet, BLUE are the dreams
you dream all alone.

PURPLE is royalty,
majestic and true;
PURPLE is midnight's
departure from blue.

velvet and berries
are violet in tone;
PURPLE is the rage of
frustration, like stone.

BROWN is rustic,
earthy, complete;
the color of cabin log
in a forest retreat.

the fur of a squirrel,
the hide of a doe,
corduroy, tweed,
tree bark… and woe.

BLACK is night time,
the sleeping soul;
disappointed loss of
a life-long goal.

BLACK is finality
ruthless and cruel;
the clamp of reality
not taught in school.

BLACK is beautiful,
it's history, it's diverse.
It's the solid-strong closing
of a color-filled verse.

BLUE & GREENS

Blue Funk Mood Music

I'm in a funk; my ship has sunk. Feeling punk.

In the mood for something, not sure what.

I'll listen to some jazz, some blues,

to lift my spirits. It always works.

> I sway to the beat, feel the heat go down to my feet.
>
> Pretty soon, feeling better, even smiling.
>
> Back to work. Energy returned.
>
> The musky notes have pulled me from the shallows.

With jaunty teal, I'm ready to heal. So surreal.

Cool aqua, powdery blue, strength of cobalt.

Midnight, royal, and navy.

Sky hues, funky moods, tonal blues: all strong, we get along.

3 Greens

Green are the leaves, climbing the branch,
and unripe tomatoes on a western ranch.

Green is beer, at the town pub in March,
to quench the thirst of throats which are parched.

The shamrock is green. I and the leprechaun, too,
wish a happy St. Pat's Day to you!

WHAT DO COLORS SAY?

Blonde hair says fun girl

Silver lining says good result

Golden touch says success

Black dress says sexy

Black suit says power

White wash says deception

Yellow-bellied says coward

Gray face says shock

Pink ribbon says breast cancer awareness

Beige says neutral

Brown says conservative

Red says blushing

Pinko says communist

Green says money

Blue says depression

Purple says royal

White says purity

Yellow says sunshine

SKY BLUE PINK

The changing sky shows

streaks of perky pink

across a canvas of palest blue,

often with free-form swabs of gray.

The pink in that sky is gentle

and seen no place else.

The pink and the blue are residents, but

blue is the host and pink is the guest.

The pink declares strong femininity

against the soft masculine blue.

Gray is the catalyst harmonizing them.

Sky blue pink smiles down on us.

HOURS OF YELLOW

12:00 midnight

I once heard someone say that yellow is the color of indecision, the one that people choose when they can't make up their minds, when they want to be safe—not too noticed, and gentle with themselves. they shun the severity of black and the boldness of red, even the welcome of green. maybe they will come back later and choose something else. yellow won't criticize them, and so they are OK with it. you can be too.

3:00 a.m.

if you let the sun of yellow enter your heart, your body, and your soul, you are fueled by its energy through the night, by its power at any hour. it is cumulative, and the more you socialize with it, the stronger you become. keep it tucked into bed with you, keep the sun more in your mind than on your body. stay in touch.

"just how do i go about this?" you might ask. "sunshine is not exactly my next door neighbor or my co-worker." answers: think about it, look at it, feel it. consider how you can interact with it. describe it to yourself on different days for varying observations. heed the variety and appreciate it.

6:00 a.m.

invite the sunshine into your attitude, into your efforts to accomplish something on your agenda, into your interactions with others. don't tell them it is there—your secret. march it in your steps as you enter your day. let your legs and feet become empowered by its strength. bask it its beauty. smile at it. meditate with it. see it with your eyes closed.

9:00 a.m.

having a relationship with brassy sunshine is a warm and warming experience, no pun intended. really. keep it close when your life becomes too noisy. let yellow be the calming influence. the voice of reason. the small, skinny voice of conscience. the one you can't ignore despite your best efforts. permit it to be your sentry and your strength. its reputation of weakness is faulty.

12:00 noon

feed your yellow. toss it around. tickle it. take it seriously but not too seriously. keep it as your friend, invest in it. take roll call of its agents: bumble bees, corn, dandelions, grosgrain hair ribbon, perfect rose in a vase on the kitchen table or lying reverently on a grave. butter. taste the yellow in your mood. a silk *cravat*. a lemon. smile, now. yellow loves you. love it back.

Nutrition?
Menu, Please

"Words are the food of a poet's soul."

— *R.F. Dorn*

Cartoon: Garfield takes a huge slice of chocolate cake on a small plate out of the fridge and says innocently, "Looks like a green salad to me!"

— *Jim Davis,* **cartoonist**

"In wine there is wisdom, in beer there is strength, in water there is bacteria."

— *David Auerbach*

"The only time to eat diet food is while you're waiting for the steak to cook."

— *Julia Child*

"The secret of success in life is to eat what you like and let the food fight it out inside."

— *Mark Twain*

"One cannot think well, love well, sleep well, if one has not dined well."

— *Virginia Woolf*

"My weaknesses have always been food and men — in that order."

— *Dolly Parton*

ICE CREAM IN THE MORNING

Eat ice cream in the morning;
let its smoothness spill all over you.
Absorb the sugar to sweeten your mood;
make it cool your heated temper.

Eat ice cream in the morning—
be greedy, but savor it;
eat when you need it.
Ice cream doesn't live by the clock.

One who eats ice cream in the morning says,
"I can do what I please.
I'm not bound by tradition.
I'll feed my soul with the cold and the smooth,
whenever it calls me."

Nuts and chocolate chips and bits of fruit
rebel against the quiet fluidity of ice cream,
against the well-behaved roundness of a scoop and
free spirited hills and caves of the ice cream in the box.

Ignore this civil war, and
eat ice cream in the morning, anyhow.

COOKIE CRUMBS

Brush those cookie crumbs out of my hair,

wipe that chocolate off my shirt;

rinse that licorice from my cheek, dear,

shake that sugar off my skirt.

Flick those cupcake chunks away from me—

I'm supposed to be on a diet,

but now that you're my baby,

I know that you'll keep quiet!

FAVORITE FOOD EXPERIENCES

Champagne and caviar on toast in his apartment,
      at midnight, on our first New Year's Eve

Breakfast in bed, served by my husband and children,
      one long ago Mother's Day

Morning afters: a. doggie-bagged Chinese food for breakfast
                    b. lobster pizza from the night before
                    c. the remaining few BBQ ribs

Eating ice cream in bed after making love,
      replacing the post-sex cigarette of years earlier

As a child, licking the mixing bowl after my mom put the cake
      in the oven; didn't really lick the bowl-- I used a spoon.

One piece of bittersweet chocolate, refrigerator-chilled

Eating buttery popcorn at the movies; sometimes our fingers
      touch when we dive into the bag at the same moment

A spoonful of sweet yellow corn, out of the pot, just boiled

First bite of a cold, jumbo shrimp, from an elegant platter, at
      a fancy buffet

Slowly slicing an avocado for guacamole, salivating at the
      thought of how good it will taste in a few minutes

Frozen grapes, eating them purposefully, one at a time

Marinated artichokes, from Trader Joe's in Sherman Oaks, CA

Matzoh ball soup: hot, smooth, seasoned with tradition

NINETTE

Syllables by stanza: 1-9 and 9-1

Salt
sugar
fatty foods
potatoes fried
sweet, moist, and tasty
deep in the frying pan
all must stay far, far away
from me—not my fault they cause fat;
now just what do you think of all that?

A lettuce salad, green and crispy:
creamy dressing but labeled "lite"
cukes serrated on edges
one radish or a few
for me; some for you.
healthy choices.
you think so?
maybe
not.

MANNERS BIG BOY

Manners Big Boy was a casual, family restaurant
in Cleveland, Ohio— a popular spot in the friendly 1950's.
You could drive through, then a new, novel feature, or eat
      inside where it was bright, festive, and noisy with fun.
      The cheerful, chubby-cheeked face of Big Boy
      perched atop the building to greet prospective guests.

The giant glossy cardboard menu featured the Big Boy burger,
in several size and content variations, of course.
Also tempting were the usual accompaniments:
      Fries, cole slaw, Cokes, shakes, and apple pie ala mode.
      No sign of green salad, vegetarian, gluten-free, or low
      calorie items.

Manners Big Boy was a place where you came to eat with a large crowd,
a few friends, maybe a casual date. No diets, no restrictions, no issues.
Just order up, drink and eat your fill, talk and laugh.
      The medium Big Boy was so huge that even a grown
      man had to open his mouth wide to get a full bite; the
      rest of us did the best we could. Of course, the French
      fries were long, thick, and salty, and we dipped them
      unstintingly into round little cups of red ketchup.

The smiling waitresses (no waiters) were upbeat and called everyone
"Honey." All the food was yummy; we gave no thought to weight
control, cholesterol, or high blood pressure, and somehow we survived.
It was a time of carefree indulging.
      When I think of a food fave from my childhood,
      Manners Big Boy flirtatiously smiles from my memory
      and calls out, "Hi, there, remember me and all the good
      times we had together?" Yes, I sure do.

THE FACES OF PIZZA

I. Pizza is what you get in the Italian restaurant
      on a rainy night, with your buddies from the office.
Pizza is what you eat the next morning for breakfast,
      when your team couldn't finish
      the six supreme specials the night before.
Pizza is what you order in when friends drop by, and
      no one feels like cooking or driving.

II. Pizza is what you bring home after a rough day at work,
      when you need a treat.
Pizza is what you create in your own kitchen, having learned
      how at your last gourmet cooking class.
Pizza sits on the table between the two of you; red candle,
      bottle of Chianti, and love songs in the background.

III. Pizza is what you eat alone when you are pigging out,
      on a "screw-the-diet" binge.
Pizza is what the kids request at the arcade birthday party.
Pizza from the freezer is an impromptu snack.

IV. Pizza is what you give up for Lent.
Pizza with only green pepper and olives on the cheese is vegetarian.
Pizza is nutritious: carb and protein.

V. Pizza is how you celebrate a promotion, good grades,
       or the completion of chemotherapy.
Pizza is your energy source when studying for finals.
Pizza is what you eat with beer while watching the Super Bowl!

Pizza is an ethnically global food;
       its face comes in different sizes and vibrant colors;
       it responds to your varied moods.
Its profile is attractive, and it has universal appeal.
       That's what pizza is!

WEATHER REPORT

"Raindrops keep falling on my head…."

— Burt Bacharach

"If you want to see the sunshine, you have to weather the storm."

— Frank Lane

"Wherever you go, no matter what the weather, always bring your own sunshine."

— Anthony J. D'Angelo

"When you walk through a storm, hold your head up high and don't be afraid of the dark…."

— Richard Rogers and Oscar Hammerstein

"April showers bring May flowers, but August rains bring hurricanes."

— Unknown

"Hold fast to dreams,
For when dreams go,
Life is a barren field,
Frozen with snow."

— Langston Hughes

ANTICS OF THE WIND

Wind in the willows
wind in the air
lifts ants off the ground
sends bees through my hair.

The wind tiptoes on my neck
and whips 'round my face
speeds up and down my arms
as if in a corporate 5K race.

The wind in a hurricane
is vicious and brash
causing branches to break
and windows to crash.

The wind taps gold sunflowers
so bright in the field
then pokes poison ivy
until its leaves are revealed.

HURRICANE MOVES

In a hurricane storm, stay safe and warm.

Be indoors and dry; don't cry.

     I see a hurricane, not arcane, but a cause of strain.

     More than a scowl, but an angry howl.

Eat bread and butters; glad you put up those shutters?

"Let it rain, let it rain" was a popular refrain.*

     Ignore the sea food ban; make tuna salad from a can;

     forget conditioning of the air or blow drying of your hair.

Neighbors invite us to a hurricane bash:

"Bring soda, batteries, chips, corned beef hash."

     We listen to the wind wreaking havoc and rage

     on our house, in our 'hood, a vicious rampage.

A hurricane is a royal pain,

but when it's over, we'll go outside and play Red Rover!

Song written by British rock musician Eric Clapton in 1970.

SITTING IN THE RAIN

I'm sitting in the rain, . . .

getting soaking wet . . . .

conjuring up some thoughts—

a poem to beget.

    Trying to construct an ode

    from within my soul;

    being fed by rain

    makes me want to stroll.

Finally I catch the words,

and 'though they're somewhat damp,

put together, they succeed

in warming me like a lamp.

MISTY CLOUDS

The misty clouds up in the sky

are friendly shapes, waltzing by.

The misty clouds, baby blue and chalky white,

form lambs and baby faces, castles candle-bright.

The misty clouds at balmy end of day

introduce a dark'ning sky and continue on their way,

only to return with sunshine's next appearance

and send down cleansing rain — Heaven's water clearance!

RAINY NIGHT REFLECTIONS

A rainy night is a chance to put on flannel jammies,
crawl into bed, and read a book, watch TV, eat chocolate,
sleep, dream, regret, fantasize

or to take a walk in the cool drops and think, sing, empty your mind,
listen to the sounds of the dark, feel the shapes,
heed the music of your own footsteps and change their cadence.
Smell the wet, be kissed by the breeze.

A rainy night is time to bake cookies or make stew, write a story,
repair a broken object, re-organize your desk or workshop,
call an old friend and a new one, work out, take a vow,
listen to jazz, meditate.

A rainy night presents us with the gift of minutes
to refresh and replenish, moments to reflect,
and to decide whether to keep walking the path we are on
or to change directions.

A night of rain lets us do all that.

THE SEA'S AGENDA

The sea has an agenda all of its own,

traveling and ever returning home.

      The places it visits are not hard to conceive:

        distant climes and shores, with no wish to deceive.

It holds swimmers and waders and motor boaters,

water skiers, surfboarders, and ray-catching floaters.

      Seasoned by salt of the very best kind;

        occupied by fish who surely don't mind.

Pebbles and stones and algae-green seaweed;

Coast Guard vessels doing their daily good deed.

      In lunar light, the waves dim morosely;

        the moon and the tide are related so closely.

Viewing the sea, I stand still on the shore,

musing how its life is filled with lore

      of history, and treasure from pirates so tough.

      Sometimes it's gentle, other times rough.

The sea touches years of the past and modernity,

fulfilling its purpose, for all eternity.

ENVIRONMENTAL HAIKU

Rushing rain drops crash

to earth in a torrent of

exhaustion, all spent.

Listening to the

grass grow, ants bite, sun shine on

the pasture, in peace.

Snow men, snow women

smile in the frigid weather,

sadly melt in warmth.

Wind Traveler

Tree branches sway
in tune with the wind,
each night and day;
we pay them no mind.

The wind whispers through
trees' large, empty spaces;
it tries hard to do
what it must, in high places.

Down it swirls, burning,
in its maelstrom of mirth;
the wind is returning
to the comfort of Earth.

Whispers goodbye to the tree
and swings back home, to the sea.

WHO IS THE SUN?

What relationship have you with the sun?

He could be your buddy, your predator, your vacation must-have.

He wants to brighten your mood when he shows up early one morning

Don't be oblivious to his gifts of warmth and cheer but

      avoid his dangerous rays at all costs.

Have you fallen out of love with a sun tan?

      Probably a healthy decision.

Remember the pale swim suit straps on your back

      from childhood days at the beach?

Notice the sparkle of a raindrop

      with sunshine acting as its tiara.

The gardener in you looks up at the sky and encourages the sun to

      come and feed your plants and flowers.

Be grateful that sun rather than rain has attended your picnic.

Think about the sun.

Don't ignore him. He is watching you.

SOCIAL COMMENTARY

"You must not lose faith in humanity. Humanity is an ocean; if a few drops of the ocean are dirty, the ocean does not become dirty."

— *Mahatma Gandhi*

"Where justice is denied, where poverty is enforced, where ignorance prevails, and where any one class is made to feel that society is an organized conspiracy to oppress, rob and degrade them, neither persons nor property will be safe."

— *Frederick Douglass*

"Friends are the family you choose."

— *Jess C. Scott,* **The Other Side of Life**

"Moral certainty is always a sign of cultural inferiority. The more uncivilized the man, the surer he is that he knows precisely what is right and what is wrong. All human progress, even in morals, has been the work of men who have doubted the current moral values …."

— *H.L. Mencken*

"In individuals, insanity is rare; but in groups, parties, nations, and epochs, it is the rule."

— *Friedrich Nietzsche*

"If everyone demanded peace instead of another television set, then there'd be peace."

— *John Lennon*

CIRCLE OF INFLUENCE

Friends from this country and those from afar—
all of them, with me, are on par.

Friends of my faith and other than mine
at my table may comfortably dine.
  Friends who are gay, bi, transgender, or straight
  are welcome to walk through my open gate.

Friends whose politics toast another party
will receive a greeting that's civil, if not hearty.
  Friends who are elderly and who are younger
  may share their views, for which I hunger.

Friends with skin black, brown, red, white, or yellow
will always hear in my home a friendly "Hello."
  My life will be flavored by these varied hues,
  and I'll be enriched by their global views.

Thus, my circle of influence will be diverse,
and we'll all be better off, surely not worse.

STREET CORNER

deep drag on the cigarette and a slow exhale

leather jacket's soft creases

exchanging curse words, but with affection

watching the skirts trot by

messages in raised eyebrows, understood

loud guffaws

keeping an ear out for the cops

eyes squinting

checking out cool wheels passing

boots shifting edgily

hungry for something, not sure what.

ignoring the issue, but coming back to it.

ignoring it again

PLAYGROUND

Several kids are climbing on the Jungle Gym; one falls off.

Two boys laugh raucously and point fingers.

Two girls come over and say, "Are you ok?" "We'll help you up."

The teacher appears and asks, "Who knocked Pat off the Jungle Gym?"

The four kids all report, "Nobody did—Pat's just clumsy."

The teacher insists that there must be a culprit.

"If you don't tell me who it was, everyone will get punished."

"That's not fair," the other four all protest.

"Well, that's the way it's going to be," the teacher insists.

The two boys begin to cuss; the two girls begin to cry.

Pat has now gotten up and walked away.

The teacher threatens to call their mothers,

dragging the four kids with her toward the school building.

"I don't have a mom," says one. "She died last year."

"I don't have one either," says another, "but I have two dads."

"I have a mom but you can't call her because my parents are divorced
and she lives in another country."

"I have a mom," says the fourth kid, "but she's deaf.

Do you know sign language, Teacher?"

Pat yells from across the playground, "It was Lee, this kid right here
who pushed me. Punish Lee, Teacher! Punish Lee!"

TATTOO COLLAGE

i. The neon sign says *Tattoos by Lou;*
seductively, it winks at you.

A current fad, a decorative art,
a fashion statement: a blue and red heart
beribboned by streamers,
dwelt on by dreamers
committed to the core
who are in love, "forevermore!"

Here's what Lou can do for you: Inscribe a trend
on your ankle, wrist, or on your rear end.

He lets the world know that you weren't afraid,
that you're wild and crazy and not a bit staid.
A pirate's face in the dark of night,
a rocky skull above crossed bones,
neatly stitched sampler saying,
"Home Sweet Home."
A racing car with your number on it,
a motorcycle with you upon it,
a butterfly, rose, star that you deem,
a rainbow with a golden sunbeam!

ii. Tattoo: a permanent reminder of a temporary feeling

— *Unknown*

iii. "My body is my journal, and my tattoos are my story."

— *Johnny Depp*

iv. Tattoos speak of you to the world the way a T-shirt does,
and you never have to put it in the washing machine!

— *Anonymous*

STANDING ON THE FENCE

standing on the fence,
looking to the left and looking to the right,
gazing at the girl and gazing at the guy,
checking out her chest straining 'neath her sweater,
checking out his buff bod, through his skimpy tank,
noticing the girl fluttering her lashes,
noting as the guy gently touched his hip.

standing on the fence,
not sure which way to jump.
eyeing the guy and ogling the girl,
attracted by her fragrance, the scent of yellow roses,
attracted to the fellow's neatly crew-cut hair,
liking how she walks, calmly, one foot before the other,
loving how he'd flex his muscles, showing off their shape.

straddling the fence,
thinking of being on one side and on the other,
gazing far across the fence, wishing also to be there,
to put an arm around her shoulder softly,
to clasp his hand and hold it warmly,
standing on the fence, trying to decide
onto which side of it to jump.

JEWELRY STORY

Rings on her fingers, diamond in her nose,
gold hoops in his earlobes. Anything goes.

A thin curved wire edges her eyebrow;
this decorative touch says, "Notice me, now!"

Tongue stud shines when he opens his lips,
but gets all milky when a shake he sips.

Head shaven closely, tattoo on his skull,
nipple balls dangle; no body part's dull.

Her belly button is fully adorned
with a sparkly gem; that's how it's worn.

A Prince Albert circle of golden yellow;
so exotic; never gets old on this fellow.

Guiche ring crafted of sterling silver
makes promises it's sure to deliver.

Body jewelry tells a tale of its own—
it speaks and sings; the wearer is never alone.

TRIO

1968. What Lies Ahead?

What lies ahead for a town where they kill
for disagreement of political will?
       Where is the value of beauty and truth,
       if hatred and violence infect our youth?
What happens to love for friends and for kin,
if murder ensues due to color of skin?

1986. Across the City

Across the city in shades of night
occur some actions that are a blight.
       Beatings and killings and rampant crime
       all contribute to the city's grime.
Shootings and theft, kidnapping, rape,
abuse, and neglect leave us agape.
       What can be done, (it isn't pretty),
       to clean up our streets in this crime-ridden city?
What can we do beside whimper and whine?
strong action is needed; it's long past time.

2004. Differences

Differences cause problems in many heinous ways,
filling with grief and conflict man's precious few days.
       If only our differences could be used to enrich,
       we'd live in harmony, each secure in a niche.
But we cut off a hand for a piece of land,
and murder a brother because of his color,
       and not join forces to steady our courses;
       need a common goal to reach a peaceful role.

THANKING + GIVING

Thanks for people: family, and friends,
for a loving relationship that never ends.

For food, for job, and for our home
that gives us a spot so we don't have to roam.

For body and mind to be in good health;
and, to cover our needs, sufficient wealth.

For a sunny outlook on life
toward parents, kids, husband, and wife.

For the strength to endure
what optimism alone won't cure.

Giving away something to another:
a neighbor, a stranger, a sister, or brother.

Maybe it's food, patience, money, or time,
or gratitude to a higher power, divine.

Giving attention to ourselves for what we need;
for someone less fortunate, doing a good deed.

Nourishing our planet to make it stronger
so it will support us a little bit longer.

Giving thanks and thankful giving—
improving the lot for we who are living.

AGE, AGES, & TIME

"Youth is the gift of nature, but age is a work of art."
— *Stanislaw Jerzy Lec*

"Age appears to be best in four things:
1. old wood to burn
2. old wine to drink
3. old friends to trust
4. old authors to read."

— *Francis Bacon*

"The old believe everything, the middle-aged suspect everything, the young know everything."
— *Oscar Wilde*

"Do not go gentle into that good night but rage, rage, against the dying of the light."
— *Dylan Thomas*

"Youth has no age."

— *Pablo Picasso*

"Time and tide wait for no man."
— *Geoffrey Chaucer*

"Don't spend time beating on a wall, hoping to transform it into a door."

— *Coco Chanel*

IN MY THOUGHTS

Some evening when I am quite alone
sittng near my window, very still
beneath the whiteness of the moon,
you enter the salon of my thoughts.
You do so silently and sightlessly—
no one but I can know your presence.

I wait for your words,
which I do not hear, but feel.
The wisdom that we share is ours alone,
a treasure that only we have made.
And when you leave,
your essence remains with me forever.

Inspired by Humbert Wolfe's The White Dress

SUMMER OF MY DISCONTENT

It was the summer of my discontent.
At 14, off to summer camp I went.
>> And when I got there I fell in love. . .
>> totally, like a true turtle dove.

His name was Alfie, 16, a counselor so cute;
all nervous around him, I was mute.
>> When he was near, I sweated and giggled;
>> at night in bed, I dreamed of him and wiggled.

He teased me by saying, "RF, I love her,"
but confessed actress Rhonda Fleming was his cover.
>> Well, the two weeks flew by and I had to go home,
>> but there was no living with me—I was a gnome.

I told my parents "I must go back
to see him some more." I would take no flack.
>> So my parents caved and gave me two more weeks,
>> knowing full well my heart still might leak.

Of that summer, this was Week #7
and, at the start it was totally Heaven—
>> he was surprised to see me there
>> and at first offered a friendly air.

But you know the game—
it wasn't at all anymore the same.
>> He hardly ever joked with me,
>> and I was devoid of any glee.

To my despair, the magic went flat—
I no longer thought he was "all that."
      I felt sad I had imposed on my parents' good will;
      of happiness they wanted to give me my fill.

Not sure what I learned from two camp trips that summer:
I came home tanned and fit; it still was a bummer.
      Maturity always includes some strife;
      I guess growing up is part of life.

WICKED WEDNESDAY

Wicked Wednesday has arrived and I

lie awake beneath the midnight sky.

Up for hours, nocturnal sentinel of dark,

I guard the moon and stars until the lark

ascends upon the light of day.

Another calendar number eaten away.

JUST TOOLING ALONG

January is tooling along, singing its song,
of "Once upon another year."
The future will usher in, in its stead,
thrills, peace, and some dollops of fear.

Plusses and minuses, gains and losses,
friends, enemies, strangers, and bosses.
Days of laughter, nights of gloom,
moments when we want to move to the moon.

Find something funny, when it rains or is sunny,
in every single thing we do.
So hail our convictions, avoid restrictions,
and let our annual dreams come true.

NO, I WON'T GO GENTLY. . .

No, I won't "go" gently "into that good night."
Why should I?
What makes anyone think it's good?
And how would they know?
Besides it's not night, anyway—it's death.
A bit of a difference there, I might add, metaphor or not.

Death with dignity? Nonsense!
Life is dignified enough for me, thank you.
Life and I have become great friends. We're very close.
We're real used to each other by now.

Tubes and machinery are objects of art, dignified art.
If they can save my life, even maybe,
I have no problem with them.
I'm not prejudiced against the minority called "Medical Technology"
or against the religion of "Life Support Systems."
Let them keep doing CPR on me until it goes out of style.
If they haven't found a cure for whatever is trying to kill me, I'll wait.
I'm in no rush to go anywhere—gently or not.

And if I am forced to go, I'll go kicking and screaming.
Life is precious. Life is all. I believe in it.
I'll not abandon my belief without a fight.
No sir, I'll not go gently into that dark night,
I'll not go gently there or anywhere else.

In updated total agreement with Dylan Thomas's premise,
in Do Not Go Gentle into That Good Night.

ON BEING 70

I never thought about me being 70, when I was younger and young.

70 was for gray-haired grandparents, elderly neighbors, and politicians.

Then it was for parents.

But the grandparents and the elderly neighbors grew older and they died.

The politicians lost the elections.

Then the parents grew older and they died.

Now we are 70. Uh oh. Are we in trouble?

No.

We still drive, party, read, write, jog, travel, surf the web, surf the waves,

dance, think, and do lots of good stuff.

We look pretty good and feel OK.

So 70 must be different than it used to be. . . . . . . so far, anyhow.

RETIRE AND WAIT FOR DEATH?

first they "retire" from their jobs.
then sell the house for smaller quarters.
rent out the condo, move to an ALF.
stop playing bingo and going in to dinner.
they sit around, just waiting to die.
no, i won't do that.

i have books to write and trips to take,
parties to dance at and cookies to bake,
business meetings i must attend,
a few relationships to mend,
my hair to color and clothes to buy.
i'm not ready to retire and wait to die.

a few more paychecks i can earn,
more golden goals for which i yearn,
some fancy dinners left to host,
new achievements of which i'll boast,
5K races for me to run,
and poetry contests which i'll have won,
friends to visit and family to see—
all them warmly waiting for me.

i don't have the time to die,
too busy eating corned beef on rye.
i won't nibble at Death's dangling bait;
He and i do not have a date.
i have much more of Life to see;
Death will have to wait until i'm free,
which, of course— I'll never be.

SONNET OF AGE

How did I ever reach this advanced age?

By living each moment, one day at a time.

The decades were filled with joy and rage,

and I could always pen a rhyme.

The years flowed, like a trickling stream,

nourishing my heart and my soul.

Some months were a nightmare, others a dream.

A few weeks were fragmented; others were whole.

Reviewing the pages of my life, so far,

I cry and laugh and deeply feel

that most of them glow like a star

'though certain ones I would repeal.

I am the many portraits of my life:

writer, friend, sister, mother, wife.

REMEMBRANCE OF THINGS PAST

(Thanks for the title, Marcel Proust)

1. Paradiddle, Flammadiddle

My father, **David Fidler**, was the youngest of Rose and
Philip's three children, born in Warsaw, Poland, but raised
in Brooklyn, New York.
His siblings were Ruth, the eldest,
whose claim to fame was being the girl
and Sam, who was a musician (a pianist)
like their father Philip (violinist = fiddler).

David wanted to learn to play the drums, so
his father took him to a colleague for lessons.
Tactlessly, the man reported that "David has no ear,"
that is, no talent.
Thus, Philip took David home and said he could not study.
He would not give David lessons just so he could enjoy the
drums, which fascinated him, and perhaps develop "an ear."

Fast forward about 35 years. Cleveland, Ohio.
When my brother Eric was in high school, he played
the drums in the marching band and our dad David sat
in on the private lessons.
When Eric graduated from college and went out into the world,
he left the big drum set at my parents' home and David finally
had his chance.

He and my mom, Bea, on the piano, had their own little
jam sessions; they played for themselves, family, and
friends, who often sang along. I'm so happy you could
check that one off on your bucket list, Dad. Yay!!!

2. Words of Wisdom

My mother, **Beatrice Greenberg Fidler**, (called Bea or Beattie, Mom, and later by her grandsons Grandma Bea or Bea Babe) being a typical mother, gave me advice at different stages of my life, each one with urgency. Here are some of the ones I remember:

a- If you can't say something nice about someone, don't say anything at all.

b- Act like a lady. (Ladies don't chew gum.)

c- Don't do anything behind my back that you would be ashamed to do in front of me.

d- Telling a lie or cheating is just as bad as stealing.

e- Always tell your parents the truth; don't keep any secrets from us.

f- Stand up straight, and smile!

g- Wear clean underwear every day. . . . even though nobody will see it.

h- Take your parents' advice; they will never steer you wrong.

i- Always turn your homework in on time.

j- Arriving late for an appointment shows your disrespect for the other person.

k- I once had an argument with a close friend in high school. That week our club meeting was scheduled to be at my house and she was in the club. I asked my mom what I should do about Karen, when she arrived, as we weren't speaking to each other. My mom said, "You will greet her politely and treat her graciously, because when she comes to your home, she is your guest."

P.S. The words of wisdom I still recall from my father were " Short term sacrifice for long term gain."

THE JUGGLER

She juggles medicine for the pain in her neck with
      the damage it does to her kidneys.

She juggles cold toes with
      the twist that bending down to put on sox gives her hips.

She juggles more pills to suppress her cough with
      the dizziness it causes.

She juggles the cost of a pedicure with
      relief from an ingrown toenail, which she can't reach to cut.

She juggles fatigue with
      the displeasure of a messy room.

She juggles trying to remember an elusive thought with
      the dismay of trying to do so.

She juggles irritation of all this effort with
      the gratitude that she is still alive.

SELFIES

"Trust yourself. Create the kind of self that you will be happy to live with all your life. Make the most of yourself by fanning the tiny, inner sparks of possibility into flames of achievement."

— *Golda Meir*

"There is only one corner of the universe you can be certain of improving, and that's your own self."

— *Aldous Huxley*

"Be yourself, but always your better self."

— *Karl G. Maeser*

"The ultimate mystery is one's own self."

— *Sammy Davis, Jr.*

"The 'self-image' is the key to human personality and human behavior. Change the self image and you change the personality and the behavior."

— *Maxwell Maltz*

"I count him braver who overcomes his desires than he who conquers his enemies, for the hardest victory is over self."

— *Aristotle*

DON'T BREAK HER RULES

Beware of this teacher, soft and sweet;
mistakes she's made, she won't repeat.

She loves to partake in verbal duels,
but has a set of stringent social rules.

Regard this teacher, surprises are her aim;
she could blow the whistle in the middle of the game.

It may appear that silly tricks she likes to play,
and she might grow sour, not getting her own way.

So play it slow; don't be cool.
But most of all, don't break her rules!

I Never Thought
That I Was Real

I never thought that I was real—
is that why it takes me so long to heal?

I see my life as just a dream;
things are not always what they seem.

Everyone else exists in one tight group,
bound by a huge, strong, powerful loop,

and I live imprisoned alone, in another.
Only ones who almost got in were my father and my mother.

I find the world divided in two
and never feel connected to

the rest of humanity,
because they mirror themselves and I see me.

What makes them all the same
is that they do not have my name,

and I am the only one who
views life exactly from my point of view.

SOME DAYS

Some days I just don't know who I am.

Like today, I ate white bread with butter and jam

and walked, aimlessly, about the house,

as if I were a catless mouse.

Took several naps and ate chocolate truffles

in my PJs and fluffy slipper shuffles.

Talked very little but coughed a lot;

remembered some stuff, but mostly forgot.

Energy and ambition contrived to escape from me

but cloaks of lethargy fully endraped me.

MILESTONE BIRTHDAY

As I reach a milestone birthday and still thrive,
I should be grateful I'm still alive,
although I may sometimes yearn
to again be 25; yes, I would return.

Younger face, body, and brain function too,
are losses which I sometime rue.
But mostly I lust for, as I lie in my bed,
the many years that then waited ahead.

Expectations, a big future, and lots of hope
are absentees with which I now must cope.
And yet to be honest and perfectly true,
I've now riches about which I then had no clue:

Dignity, confidence, pride in whom I've become:
no longer pushable under somebody's thumb.
Like to think I'm a better and kinder soul. . .
gentle with others, I try to make them feel whole.

As I ponder posterity and leaving my mark,
maybe the future, after all, isn't so dark.
Although I've some aches and take a few pills,
the Health Fairy has brought me no serious ills.

I'm blessed with 1 husband, 2 sons, 2 daughters-in-law,
and 2 gorgeous grandchildren, whom I view with awe.

Another valued gift that is precious to me
are cherished friends—those in my social family.
My writer pals are grand people to know, as I age;
when we're together, we're on the same page.

Since I plan to live to 120, maybe this age isn't so old;
each year's a treasure, more valuable than silver or gold.

CLIMB INTO THE BED

i climb into the bed
and cover up my head;
woolly blankets and percale sheets
tangle in a rhythm, as my heart beats.
restlessly, i smooth the case of my pillow;
through open window, rustles a branch of a willow.

the warmth here in the room,
recalls my time within the womb,
where i was safe from all harm,
had no cause for any alarm.
where i was snug and secure
with no trials to endure.
now i turn and then i toss. . .
wondering, did i floss?

pull my arms in close to my chest,
let my knees bend slightly, ready for rest,
then snuggle cozily way down deep;
emit a sigh before falling asleep,
submitting to dreams
of valleys and streams,
until morning smiles and visit from Morpheus ends;
blankets and sheets: two nocturnal friends.

ROLLER COASTER

My life is such a roller coaster:
skyscraper highs and sandpit lows.
When I'm up I think I'll be there forever.
When I'm down I fear I'll never leave.

Any time I foolishly think I can control the trip,
the speed, the direction, the destination, whoosh!!
The little cart scoops me up and whisks me away
to a spot of its own choosing. Most certainly not mine.

And I am like the passenger in the kidnap car.
Control? Choices? Ha. Not a prayer.
But still I keep getting surprised
each time my authority is attacked.

Since I'm not going to be the driver this time around,
guess I should just fasten my seat belt
and enjoy the ride from the passenger seat.

Printed in the United States
By Bookmasters